Barmy Ballads

Colin West

Matador
9 Priory Business Park,
Wistow Road, Kibworth Beauchamp,
Leicestershire. LE8 0RX
Tel: 0116 279 2299
Email: books@troubador.co.uk
Web: www.troubador.co.uk/matador
Twitter: @matadorbooks

ISBN 978 1838595 180

British Library Cataloguing in Publication Data.
A catalogue record for this book is available from the British Library.

Printed and bound in the UK by TJ International, Padstow, Cornwall
Typeset in 14pt Minion Pro by Troubador Publishing Ltd, Leicester, UK

Matador is an imprint of Troubador Publishing Ltd

Contents

For Cathie

The King of Cobblestone Castle

This is the King of Cobblestone Castle.

This is the page
who carries a parcel
addressed to the King
of Cobblestone Castle.

This is the mother
who serves up the supper
for the page called Paul
who carries a parcel
addressed to the King
of Cobblestone Castle.

This is the farmer
who churns the butter
to sell to the mother
who serves up the supper
for the page called Paul
who carries a parcel
addressed to the King
of Cobblestone Castle.

This is the milkmaid
who brings her best cream
to take to the farmer
who churns the butter
to sell to the mother
who serves up the supper
for the page called Paul
who carries a parcel
addressed to the King
of Cobblestone Castle.

This is the cow in a meadow so green
who gives the milkmaid all her cream
to take to the farmer who churns the butter
to sell to the mother who serves up the supper
for the page called Paul who carries a parcel
addressed to the King of Cobblestone Castle.

This is the grass that grows on the ground
where stands the cow in a meadow so green
who gives the milkmaid all her cream
to take to the farmer who churns the butter
to sell to the mother who serves up the supper
for the page called Paul who carries a parcel
addressed to the King of Cobblestone Castle.

This is the rain that falls all around
that waters the grass that grows on the ground
where stands the cow in a meadow so green
who gives the milkmaid all her cream
to take to the farmer who churns the butter
to sell to the mother who serves up the supper
for the page called Paul who carries a parcel
addressed to the King of Cobblestone Castle.

This is the King, the old King once again,
who's been caught in the rain that falls all around
that waters the grass that grows on the ground
where stands the cow in a meadow so green
who gives the milkmaid all her cream
to take to the farmer who churns the butter
to sell to the mother who serves up the supper
for the page called Paul who carries a parcel
addressed to the King of Cobblestone Castle.

This is the parcel all tied up with string
that's now been delivered at last to the King
who was caught in the rain that falls all around
that waters the grass that grows on the ground
where stands the cow in a meadow so green
who gives the milkmaid all her cream
to take to the farmer who churns the butter
to sell to the mother who serves up the supper
for the page called Paul who carried the parcel
addressed to the King of Cobblestone Castle.

And this is what he found inside:
A BRIGHT UMBRELLA TALL AND WIDE!

And now the King is far from glum
now that his birthday gift has come
a present from the Queen of Spain
to help the King keep off the rain
the rain that's falling all around
that waters the grass that grows on the ground
where stands the cow in a meadow so green
who gives the milkmaid all her cream
to take to the farmer who churns the butter
to sell to the mother who serves up the supper
for the page called Paul who carried the parcel
all of the way to Cobblestone Castle!

Sir Stinkalot

There lived a knight long years ago
Who wasn't very nice to know.
When other knights soaked in a bath
In wooden tub before the hearth,
Sir Stinkalot just shook his head
And took a book and went to bed.
O how he hated suds and soap!
The mere thought made him moan and mope.
Thus never did he wash his feet,
His hair was never nice and neat,
He never sank into a tub

To give his back a good old scrub,
Nor did he wash behind his ears,
And this went on for years and years.
And with a bath so overdue,
No wonder that his friends were few.
The dragons that he sought to slay
Surrendered when he came their way,
He left them writhing on their backs —
No need to use a battle axe —
And damsels who were in distress
Soon overcame their helplessness,
And told him things were now all right
And that they didn't need a knight.

But then the day came when he went
Into a strange establishment …

… A building that was grey and grim,
Quite irresistible to him!

Now, keen Sir Stinkalot
	had heard
That awful things
	therein occurred,
Yet all the same,
	Sir Stinkalot
Was not afraid
	of that one jot,
But entering the
	hallway dim,
A sudden change
	came over him:

He started shaking
	as with fright,
And soon he was
	a nervous knight.
Upright stood his
	plume (or feather)
Whilst his kneecaps
	knocked together.
What did he see
	to make him shake?
What made him in
	his armour quake?

The fearsome sight which filled his eyes
And gave him such a big surprise
Was seven maidens armed with mops
And buckets brimming to their tops
With disinfectant which they sloshed
All over him till he was washed!

And when they'd cleaned
   him, then they went
And soaked him in
   a vat of scent,
Which he emerged from
   smelling sweet
As roses, from his
   head to feet.

But how Sir Stinky
    hated it!
He didn't like the
    whiff a bit.
It took the best part
    of a year
For it to wholly
    disappear.

And when he was restored once more
To old Sir Stinkalot of yore,
He slipped away to find a place
Far from the horrid human race.
It's thought he found a distant cave
Where he could still be bold and brave,
And where he lived for all his time
With warthogs in the dirt and grime.

Invisible Isobel

Invisible Isobel
Crept out one night,
And thought that she'd give
All the neighbours a fright.

She banged on
    the windows
And rattled the
    bins,
And startled the
    people
With various
    dins.

She knocked
    every knocker
And rang every
    bell,
And raised such
    a rumpus
That folk couldn't
    tell

How such a great racket
Could come from nowhere,
For when they all looked,
There was nobody there!

Walter Wilde,
the Gifted Child

A prodigy was Walter Wilde,
(Which means he was a gifted child).
Just nine months after he was born,
Up he got and mowed the lawn.
He gave the garden fence a coat
(At eighteen months) of creosote,
And by the time that he was three,
He'd fixed the broken-down T.V.

Remarked his mother to her spouse,
"Our lad seems handy round the house.
We maybe should advantage take,
Think of the money we could make!"
So thus they advertised their son:
Come get your household jobs all done!

And soon they hired out little Walt,
Who proved hardworking to a fault.

He, for example,
mixed cement …

… and mended
bikes whose wheels
were bent.

He painted …

…plumbed …

… and plastered too.

There seemed no task he couldn't do.

But when he reached the age of five,
The time for schooling did arrive,
So Mummy took her Walter's hand
And walked him to the school so grand.

The teachers there were rather riled
To see such an exploited child.
They longed to educate the kid,
For after all, that's what they did.

They longed to teach him how to spell
And how to read and write as well,
To teach him how to multiply,
And all about square roots and *pi*.

But soon it was quite plain to see
An uphill struggle it would be,
So first of all, Miss Meek, the Head,
Took Walter to one side and said:

"It seems the
old school
boiler's burst.
Walt, maybe
you could fix
it first?"

The Ballad of Bertie

O, Bert worked in a circus
And swung from the trapeze.
He didn't hang on by his hands,
His ankles or his knees.

Bert had a set of dentures
(Ten above and ten beneath)
And by his twenty choppers
He hung on by his teeth.

When other trapeze artists
Swung by their arms and legs,
Bert did all his antics
Thanks to his toothypegs.

He flew this way and that way,
(And sometimes upside-down)
His face was ever smiling
And never wore a frown.

Until one day when Bertie
Upon the high trapeze
Felt that his nose was itchy
And that he'd have to sneeze.

Bert tried his best to stop it,
But as he went *Achoooo!*
He fell, but oh those dentures,
How through the air they flew!

A Witch Called Rosalind

A witch there was
called Rosalind,
whose magic broom
went like the wind.

Now see her,
cat upon her knee,
who almost was
as bad as she.

Together they would
wait till dark,
to get up to
some merry lark.

One night, whilst
flying past the palace,
the witch's heart
was filled with malice.

She swooped down on
the handsome prince,
who hasn't been
the same man since.

Ros grabbed him by
his slender hips
and kissed him *smack*
upon the lips.

And after such
a good long snog,
the prince was turned
into a frog!

But was he sorry?
No, not he,
he hopped off
happy as can be.

Still, Rosalind
could hardly care:
next week she'll change
him back. *So there!*

The Three Highwaymen

In Hampstead lived three highwaymen
As vain as they could be,
And as to who was handsomest,
They never could agree,
For each one thought, "The prettiest
Undoubtedly is *me*!"

Said Sam, "I have a noble nose
That makes me look refined!"
Said Sid, "No, it's my flaxen hair
That's always nicely shined!"
Said Saul, "No, it's my lovely eyes,
They're of the sparkling kind!"

In Hampstead thus the ruffians,
They bickered day and night,
Until at last they all agreed
To find out who was right:
They planned the hold-up of a coach,
Quite soon in broad daylight.

And furthermore, they all agreed,
To make complete the task,
When having robbed the passengers,
They'd each remove their mask,
Then, "Who's the handsomest of all?"
Their victims they would ask.

Said Sam, "I have a noble nose
That makes me look refined!"

Said Sid, "No, it's my flaxen hair
That's always nicely shined!"

Said Saul, "No, it's my lovely eyes,
They're of the sparkling kind!"

And so it was on Saturday,
Ten minutes after noon,
They stopped a coach on Hampstead Heath

And plundered from it soon.
Then, as they each pulled off their mask,
Oh, how the folk did swoon!

The highwaymen were quite perplexed
To see the people faint,
But thought, "It must be ecstasy,
The cause of this complaint.
We all three must be beautiful!"
And laughed without restraint.

And satisfied, they galloped home,
Where they spent several days
A-gazing in the mirror through
A sort of rosy haze,
And flattering each other too,
With tender words of praise.

But people soon put posters up
Enquiring, "Have you seen
Three highwaymen? One with a nose
Shaped like a runner bean?
Another who has haystack hair?
And one whose eyes look mean?"

A Romantic Yarn

Said a pair of scissors
to ball of twine,
"I like your fibre,
will you be mine?"

Said the ball of twine,
"I could never feel
love for one
whose heart is steel."

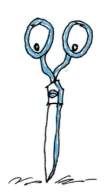

Said the pair of scissors,
"Though metal-made,
where could you find
so fine a blade?"

Said the ball of twine,
"You're trim, it's true,
but also sharp,
and I can't love you."

Said the pair of scissors,
"Is there no shred
of hope, one day,
that we might wed?"

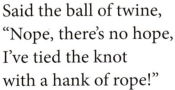

Said the ball of twine,
"Nope, there's no hope,
I've tied the knot
with a hank of rope!"

Mary the Mixed-up Mermaid

Now, once upon a time there was a mermaid
Who looked just like her sisters of the sea,
Above her tummy button being human,
Below it, being fishy as can be.

But Mary was a restless sort of mermaid,
Who didn't care for salty sea or foam,
She longed to live beside a yellow cornfield
Upon a hill, where she might feel at home.

Each night she slept beneath the dancing moonbeams,
And dreamed of picking pears and climbing trees,
She dreamed of doing cartwheels in the clover,
And keeping seven hives of honey bees.

One day upon the rocks she sat daydreaming,
When suddenly an octopus appeared.
To her amazement, up it slinked beside her,
And whispered words which sounded rather weird.

It said: *Bah Humbug! Balderdash! Baloney!*
Hey-nonny-no! Ho hum! and *Fiddle-dee!*
It then arose, and with a funny shuffle,
It wibble-wobbled back into the sea.

I can't say what those words meant that it mumbled,
But somehow Mary seemed to understand.
From that day on, she swims around contented,
And dreams no more of living on the land.

P.C. 47

In Dunstable a constable
(That's P.C. 47)
Would pound his beat on two flat feet,
Both of them size eleven.

He shone his torch on every porch
And on each darkened doorway,
No cop more thorough in the borough,
Or anywhere round *your* way.

And up and down that market town
He twirled his trusty truncheon,
And only once in eighteen months
He stopped to have his luncheon.

He took a bite, then had a fright
When munching his meat sandwich —
He saw a warlock touch his forelock
And greet another man witch.

And then the pair (he watched them there)
Commenced to pick a door lock,
He did his best to make arrest,
(Not easy with a warlock).

And things got worse (it made him curse!)
He choked upon some gristle.
Then could he blow for back-up? *No!*
He couldn't toot his whistle!

With no alarm, the thieves stayed calm,
And they picked even *more* locks.
The poor P.C. but helplessly
Could look on at those warlocks.

They stole some rings and other things
From jewellers they decluttered,
And all the time throughout the crime
The bobby coughed and spluttered.

Then with their bag filled up with swag,
They scarpered and quite vanished.
As for that cop, now deemed a flop,
To Dartmoor he was banished.

And now he stays for all his days
Holed up in deepest Devon.
Ah, pity me, because, you see,
I'm P.C. 47.

Connie and her Unicorn

Early one white winter's morn
Came Connie and her unicorn.
She knocked upon the great front door
Of greedy giant Gobblemore.
The giant, stirring in his bed,
Rubbed his eyes and scratched his head.
"Who is it dares wake Gobblemore?"
He roared whilst answering the door.

And who should stand there all forlorn,
But Connie and her unicorn.
(Now though he'd gorged the night before,
He hungered still, did Gobblemore),
Thought he, "Oh unicorns are sweet,
And how I yearn for tender meat!"
And so, "Dear child, come in!" he cried,
And thus did Connie go inside.

Her face was thin, her clothes were torn,
But plumpish was her unicorn.
"And what may you have come here for?"
Asked the sly giant Gobblemore,
And as he spoke, he noticed that
Her unicorn was nice and fat!
"I'm feeling peckish" Connie said,
"And come to beg a crust of bread.
I have no money, but I trust
You'll let me have a little crust."
Said Gobblemore, who wasn't kind
And had but one thought in his mind,
"If you've no gold to pay the debt,
Just let me have that freakish pet!"

At such a thought the girl felt sad,
Her unicorn was all she had,
But though her heart was sadly torn,
She sighed, "Farewell, my unicorn."
And with those words, she swapped her beast
For one extremely frugal feast.

Her crust of bread was far from large
And spread with just the *merest* marge.
Meanwhile the giant scoured a book
To see the nicest way to cook
A unicorn: fried, boiled or stewed,
Or grilled or baked or barbecued?

When Connie saw the giant take
Her unicorn away to bake,
At once she realised his game,
So grabbed a saucepan, and took aim,
Then flung it, hardly thinking that
She'd hit him, but she knocked him flat!

With Gobblemore now out stone cold,
Shy Connie was a bit more bold.
She dragged the giant across the floor,
Then kicked him out his own back door!

Then with her unicorn she went
And raided his establishment.
They ate up all that they could find
And didn't leave a scrap behind —
Ate every leg of beef and ham,
And every slice of bread and jam,
And every beetroot, every bean,
They even licked their platters clean,
And every goblet, every cup,
They drank them down and drank them up!

It took all day and half the night
To eat up everything in sight,
And when at last they both were sure
There really wasn't any more,
They left, full up, at crack of dawn,
Did Connie and her unicorn.

The Old Kitchen Sink

When we moved house,
we took everything —
my mother's old apron,
my auntie's fake mink,
four cups and saucers,
and one odd cuff link,
and several bottles
of Indian ink.

We took the old washstand
that was painted bright pink,
our old garden hosepipe
with many a kink,
and Granny's old bathtub,
(the one made of zinc),
and three pairs of socks
which had started to shrink.

We loaded the van
and were just on the brink
of leaving, when Grandad
remarked with a wink,
"That's the lot, now I'm sure
that we've got everyfink!"
then chuckled, "except for
the old kitchen sink!"

But Grandad's remark
made me suddenly blink,
it stirred up my mind
and I started to think
that never again
would I get me a drink
from the cold water tap
of the old kitchen sink.

The Dreamer's Favourite Hat

Upon a grassy hillside sat
The Dreamer, in his favourite hat.
He dreamed one day that he might rise
Above the hills, into the skies,
To dip and dive, and soar and swoop
Like some bird in a flying troupe.

It was from such a reverie
The Dreamer woke up suddenly,
And saw a man in starry clothes,
A wacky wizard, strange as those
You see in books or puppet shows,
Complete with beard and great big nose.

The wizard said, "How do you do!
I'll make your greatest wish come true."
Now, who could have said *no* to that?
The Dreamer, taking off his hat,
Politely said, "Upon my word,
I wish that I could be a bird!
I'd love to be a swallow or
A swift, so I could swoop and soar!"

The wizard, grinning
    like a cat,
Then took the Dreamer's
    favourite hat,
And having placed it
    on his head,
He waved his arms
    till he went red.

What happened next was really weird,
A magic-looking star appeared:
The Dreamer felt his arms grow longer,
He felt his muscles getting stronger,
But then his knees felt weak as water
As he watched his legs grow shorter.

The wizard waved a great amount
And made more stars than you could count,
And as the stars fell thick and fast,
The Dreamer was a bird at last!
His chest was decked in feathers brown,
His tummy turned to eider down.
He scarcely could believe such things
Until he flapped his new-found wings,
And found indeed that he could fly
And join the birdies up on high.

It's true he wasn't quite a swift,
More like a duck that's gone adrift,
But having never quite been slim,
A duck was good enough for him.

For hours that fine summer's day
He took part in an air display.
He soon learned how to soar and swoop,
And even did a loop-the-loop.
He flew with pigeons, flapped with geese,
And thought his joy would never cease,
Then when his wings began to ache,
He glided down to take a break.

Upon the grassy slope he landed,
But sensed at once he'd been left stranded.
The wizard with his nose and beard
Most thoughtlessly had disappeared!
The Dreamer sobbed and wondered how
He might again be human now.
What made the matter worse was that
He'd also lost his favourite hat!
He sought the wizard, but in vain,
He never saw his likes again.

For seven nights and seven days
The Dreamer followed birdlike ways:
He dined on snails and worms and flies
And glumly flew about the skies.
He cared no more to swoop or soar,
The whole thing had become a bore.

But then one day, this man-turned-duck
Had an amazing stroke of luck:
He spotted something in a tree,
And asked himself, "Hey, can it be
The favourite hat I used to wear?"
And saw it *was* as he got near!

He flew down to retrieve his hat,
Which now was tattered, squashed and flat,
The thing he gaily dusted down,
And soon reshaped its crumpled crown.
Then as he brushed its battered brim,
A hopeful thought occurred to him:
"The wizard wore this hat of mine,
Maybe some magic's left behind!"

He wildly waved the hat about,
Lo and behold! A star fell out!
"Yippee!" the Dreamer cried in glee,
"There's still some magic left for me!"

His wings grew short, his legs grew fat,
As stars, they tumbled from his hat,
And when no more fell out, why then,
He saw he was a man again!

And now the Dreamer may be found
With both feet firmly on the ground.
And as to having been a bird,
He utters not a single word,
His secret's safe, and that is that,
He keeps it underneath his hat!

Cousin Nelly

On a picnic Cousin Nelly
Demonstrated eating jelly,
And we would have been so grateful
Had she only ate a plateful,
But she scoffed at least a dozen
Helpings, did my little cousin.
Such a large amount of jelly
Took its toll on greedy Nelly.

She came over queer and queasy
And found standing far from easy,
When she tried to walk, she wobbled,
Thanks to all that she had gobbled.
As she staggered by the river
We could see her quake and quiver,
Though we cried out, "Mind the water!"
To my mother's brother's daughter,
In the creek the girl went crashing,
Followed by a lot of splashing.

On the banks we stood there thinking
That our Nelly should be sinking,
But her tummy proved so bloated
That she didn't sink, but floated.
So we hauled her from the river,
And as she began to shiver,
We prepared a celebration
Full of joy and jubilation.

All day long we danced round Nelly
Singing songs unto her belly.

O what mayhem we created
As she gradually deflated!

Percy the Pirate

When people think of pirates,
They think of strapping men,
With cutlasses and whiskers
And names like Jake or Ben.

But Percy was a pirate
More fearsome than the rest,
Although he had no muscles
Or hairs upon his chest.

For Percy's secret weapon
No brute could ever beat,
He never was without it —
His pair of smelly feet.

When he was out marauding,
His foes he would out-fox
By rapidly removing
His boots, and then his socks.

And then he'd do a handstand
And wave his feet aloft,
And so upon the ozone
The whiff would gently waft.

His victims' eyes would water,
Their noses, they would sniff,
Then forcefully the fellows
Would catch the pungent whiff.

And falling down like ninepins,
They'd all be knocked out cold,
Then Percy would relieve them
Of jewellery and gold.

Yes, Percy was the pirate
No brute could ever beat,
Who owned a ton of treasure
Thanks to his smelly feet!

Fearless Foolish Frank

A law-abiding boy was Frank
Until he thought to rob a bank.
(He hoped to get a hundred quid
To buy a load of sweets, he did!)

And so, to carry out
    this task,
He grabbed his bag
    and fixed his mask,
Then from his daddy's
    drinking cup
He filled his water
    pistol up.

And creeping out, so well disguised,
He hoped he'd not be recognised,
As down the road went fearless Frank
Towards his daddy's local bank.

It isn't hard to understand
How things went quite not as he planned.
Indeed, the cashiers laughed to see
Such poor attempt at robbery.
They confiscated from the boy
His plastic water pistol toy.
Now see them re-enact his prank,
And such a foolish boy looks Frank!

The Carpet with a Hole

Once a merchant in a market
Showed a tatty-looking carpet
To a rather foolish fellow:
It was purple, pink and yellow,
With a big hole in the middle,
(Which seemed something of a fiddle!)

But this fellow still adored it,
And could *just* about afford it,
So he with his money parted,
And that carpet soon he carted
To a faraway oasis
(One of his most favourite places)
And that carpet with a hole in
He was presently unrollin'.

It was damp and it was dusty
And it smelled a little musty,
But to that misguided fellow
It seemed mystical and mellow.
Though the middle bit was perished,
That old carpet, still he cherished,
So he thought he'd sit upon it
And compose a simple sonnet.

(Notice how the hole is fitting
Round him, in the middle sitting.)
Holey rug, you have a beauty
Far beyond the call of duty …
Thus he scribbled with his biro.
Meanwhile, somewhere south of Cairo …

There appeared a change of weather:
Little breezes blew together
And in strength they started growing
Till one MIGHTY blast was blowing!
Over rivers, over mountains,
Over pyramids and fountains,
It came swishing, it came swooshing,
Gaining strength and onward pushing,
Bending trees and blowing camels
Off their feet, the poor old mammals.

Soon it reached the foolish fellow,
Blew his fez off, made him bellow:
"Heavens! It has left my head bare!"
Then he lost that carpet threadbare!

Who'd have thought a breeze on high would
Send that holey carpet skyward?
But it did — with one great bluster
Up it flew, just like a duster!

High above, the carpet fluttered.
Back on earth the fellow muttered:
"Mercy me! It's truly tragic,
For that carpet's clearly magic!
I'd be flying single-handed
If it hadn't left me stranded,
And Aladdin I could follow
If that rug had not been hollow,
But as I composed my idyll,
I was sitting in the middle —
Where that hole was all around me —
Such calamities confound me!"

As he spoke, the carpet vanished,
And to Who-knows-where was banished.
What became of that old carpet?
Did it blow back to the market?
Was the merchant some magician
Who was on a mischief mission?
Messing with the desert breezes
Just one of his little wheezes?

(Thus these items which he dealt in
Came back to the home he dwelt in,
And each rug, first he would log it,
Then he once again could flog it!)

Or perhaps things aren't so mystic,
And the answer's more simplistic,
Namely, that the wind just blew it,
And that's all that there is to it!
Therefore, was its destination
Some far flung and strange location?

Or perhaps it was transported
Just a mile from where he'd brought it?
But that carpet in whose middle
Was a hole, remains a riddle,
Which that foolish fellow thinks is
Just as baffling as the Sphinx's!

A Donkey Tale

He rode into town on a donkey of brown
Wearing a massive sombrero.
(It's really quite rare for donkeys to wear
A hat like a gay caballero.)

And he very soon was in the saloon
And thumping the upright "Joanna".
She seemed not to mind, but funny to find
An animal act in that manner.

How loudly he brayed and swigged lemonade,
Then joined in a game of stud poker.
The cheats and the thieves had cards up their sleeves,
He did too (but only a Joker).

In no time at all he got in a brawl
With Lucky O'Toole from Kentucky.
He punched and he kicked and truly seemed licked,
Till with a left hoof he struck Lucky.

He finished his Schweppes, then retraced his steps
And met up again with his chappie.
The sun going down, he rode out of town
And hee-hawed 'cause he was so happy.

A Princess Called Pauline

There once was a princess called Pauline,
And under a tarpaulin awnin'
She sat on the shoreline each mornin'
And spent it in stretchin' and yawnin'
Whilst catching the crabs that were crawlin'
Beside her, beneath the tarpaulin.

One Sunday a fisherman trawlin'
For salmon before they went spawnin'
Caught sight of the princess called Pauline,
And just by the way she was sprawlin'
He found her completely enthrallin'

He went to her tarpaulin awnin'
Without even givin' a warnin'
And said, "You're appealin', O Pauline,
May I be forgiven for callin',
But for you I'm hopelessly fallin'!"

Still Pauline continued in yawnin'
And didn't acknowledge his fawnin'.
The fisherman, blubbin' and bawlin'
Returned to his callin' of trawlin'
As Pauline, without even stallin'
Went back to her habit appallin'
Of catchin' the crabs that were crawlin'
Beside her, beneath the tarpaulin.

The Ballad of
Barnaby Brown

In a corner of Kent where nobody went
Except the odd hiker or two,
Old Barnaby Brown would wake with a frown
And blow on his didgeridoo.

He didgeridoo'd in the morning,
He didgeridoo'd in the night,
All afternoon too, he'd didgeridoo,
He did it with all of his might.
He didgeridoo'd standing upright,
He didgeridoo'd sitting down,
And what did he do
    halfway 'twixt the two?
He didgeridoo'd, did old Brown!

He didgeridoo'd in his bathtub,
He didgeridoo'd in his bed,
On his didgeridoo he blew
and he blew,
Until he went purple and red.
He didgeridoo'd every minute,
He didgeridoo'd till he dropped,
And nobody knew but his
didgeridoo
Precisely the time that he stopped.

In a corner of Kent where nobody went
Except the odd hiker or two,
Old Barnaby Brown is buried deep down,
Along with his didgeridoo.

Here lies
Barnaby
Brown

Jeffrey the Jester

O Jeffrey was a jester,
But he wasn't very jolly,
He'd mooch around the castle grounds
Just looking melancholy.

He wouldn't greet the acrobats,
Or with the minstrels mingle,
And seldom did he cock a snook,
Or give his bells a jingle.

The King was quite impatient
And the Queen was almost frantic
For him to make some merry jape
Or get up to an antic.

But Jeffrey just would mope about
In Jester's suit and cap. "Stick
That in your pipe!" he'd tell them all,
"I do not care for slapstick!"

The humour that appealed to him
Was more sophisticated,
And slipping on banana skins
He thought was overrated.

The King and Queen soon realised
They never should have hired him,
And so one sunny afternoon
They nonchalantly fired him.

As Jeffrey left the castle gates
He vowed he'd be an actor,
So utterly convinced was he
That he had the "X" factor.

He bought a Roman outfit and
He fashioned him a fake spear,
So he could waggle it about
And quote the works of Shakespeare.

Alas! The public booed his act,
And critics put the boot in,
They pelted him with rotten fruit
For being highfalutin.

If you're like Jeff the Jester, folks,
Best not to raise an eyebrow.
It's fun to be a little smart,
But not to be *too* highbrow!

The Growl of the Pussycat

The growl of the Pussycat,
    meant to be
Like a growl at the back
    of her throat,
Just sounded funny, like
    some lovesick bunny
Who couldn't quite hit
    the right note.
An Owl (locked up in a
    cage above)
Then sang, though he
    suffered catarrh:

"O silly Pussy, O Pussy, please shove,
Please shove off to somewhere afar,
Afar,
Afar,
Please shove off to somewhere afar."

Pussy said to
    the Owl,
"Your manners
    are foul,
How nasally too
    do you sing!
If I were to
    force you
To wed, I'd
    divorce you
The moment you
    slipped on
    the ring!"

They bickered this way for many a day,
Till finally coming to blows.
Owl did what he could, and belted her good,
With a biff on the end of her nose,
    Her nose,
    Her nose,
With a biff on the end of her nose.

A pig who was willing them on for a killing
Cheered on in a voice which was shrill.
By the end of the day, both exhausted they lay,
Till a Turkey gave each one a pill.
Now, from that moment since, they have had
   to wear splints,
And take all their food with a spoon.

I can't understand why they act so off-hand,
Let's hope that they make up real soon,
    Real soon,
    Real soon,
Let's hope that they make up real soon.

Kitty Kaktus

You've heard of Wild Bill Hickok,
And you've heard of Jesse James,
Well, now here comes another one
To add to those there names.

For Kitty Kaktus is the girl
Who's put the Wild West in a whirl.
Hey, see her round her fingers twirl
Her pretty silver cane.

Now see
her riding
upside-down,

Or scare
a bear with
just a frown,

Or chase some bandits out of town
Across the desert plain.

And Kitty Kaktus, so I'm told,
When she was only eight years old,
Amassed a fortune panning gold,
She's never known to fail!

Now Kitty, who has just turned ten,
Last week lassoed a gang of men,
They'll never rob a bank again,
They're in the County Jail.

You've heard of Annie Oakley,
And you've heard of Wyatt Earp,
Now you'll remember What's-her-name,
Unless you are a twerp.

King Alphonse
and his Funny Family

King Alphonse was a rotten king,
And he was bad as anything,
He never acted as one should,
And stole the poor folks' Christmas pud.

He couldn't kick
or bat a ball,
he was no good
at sport at all.

And whenever
doing sums,
he used his fingers
and his thumbs!

He had a wife,
  Queen Ermentrude,
what people said
  of her was rude.
And then there was
  the young Prince Fritz,
the folk called them
  a bunch of twits!

Whenever they
  went out to dine,
they gobbled like
  a lot of swine.

And when they went out for a ride,
"It's sucks to you!" the kiddies cried.

No wonder, (though it sounds insulting),
Quite soon the peasants *were* revolting!

And Alphonse, Ermentrude and Fritz
Spent every day scared out their wits,
And later, tucked up in their beds,
Had nightmares they might lose their heads!

The Tale of Thomas Todd

A highwayman was Thomas Todd,
Who for a highwayman was odd.
Whenever holding up a coach,
"Would anybody like a brooch?"
He'd ask, or else, "Here, have my rings!
I've grown tired of the wretched things!"
Or even, "Take my watch and chain,
I've no wish to see them again!"
And then he'd empty out his pockets
And give away some golden lockets.

What's more, he wore,
up both his arms,
Bracelets full of lucky
charms,
Which to hard-up folk
at random,
He would selflessly
just hand 'em,
And if feeling still
more reckless,
He'd throw in a
diamond necklace,

Adding, as he fired
his pistol,
"All the stones are
finest crystal!"
He wasn't bad at all,
you see,
But full of
generosity,
Which for a highway-
man was odd,
But such a one was
Thomas Todd.

The Rhyme of Freddie Fry

Behold the youthful Freddie Fry
Who liked to watch the trains go by.
He was a very thorough lad,
He'd jot their numbers in a pad,
Then neatly add the Time and Date,
And "tut" if one was running late.

Now this young
fellow lately had
Been given by
his wealthy dad
A rather fancy
cam-er-a,
Which made him hoot
and howl "Hurrah!"

He snapped away with great delight
At almost everything in sight,
And every photograph he took
He pasted in a pretty book.

One morning Freddie thought that he
Might thus preserve for all to see
The famous Seven-twenty-two
Express train out of Waterloo,
Which daily passed his favoured spot
At seven thirty on the dot.

And so it was
he did unpack
His camera
beside the track,
And set the shutter
speed to *fast*
To snap the train
as it sped past.

As Freddie waited for the train,
A notion popped into his brain:
"How much improved the shot should be
If it could also feature *me*.
How lovely, when the loco came,
If I were also in the frame.
And furthermore, how proud of me
My generous papa would be!"

He set the button
    to *delay*
So he'd have time
    to make his way
Before the lens,
    and thus to be
Included in the
    snap, you see.

He waited then with bated breath
For that famed Waterloo Express.
At last the train came into sight,
O how the boy danced in delight.

Then knowing he
could clearly *hear*
The locomotive
puffing near,
He pressed the knob
and jumped out quick,
In good time for
the shutter's click.

Fred proved too keen, alas, alack!
He'd rashly leapt onto the track.
And yet he had the final laugh:
It made a *super* photograph.

The Song of Silas Bone

The meanest man I've ever known,
Without a doubt, is Silas Bone.
He keeps his money in a box
Secured with combination locks.
Some people say, but can't be sure,
He's got a thousand pounds or more.

He rides to town upon his bike
On almost every Friday night,
When moons are high and shops are shut,
And when he feels so off his nut
That no one ever dares to mock
The song he sings at twelve o'clock:

"My name is Mister Silas Bone,
The kindest man you've ever known.
I often gamble, often spend,
I often give and often lend.
Some people say, they can but guess,
I've only got a pound or less!"

The Nutty Knight

Sir Ben, a nutty knight was he,
Who thought, "There's no one bold as me!"
He loved Fiona, young and fair,
Who had green eyes and purple hair.

To win her over, off he went,
Although his sword was rather bent.
He spied a dragon far away
And thought, "This is my lucky day!"

He charged, but with a little laugh,
The dragon bit his sword in half.
Meanwhile, Fiona, what of she?
She acted wacky as can be.

She played the drums the whole day long
Whilst belting out a hip hop song,
When who should knock upon the door,
But brave Sir Ben, whose heart was sore.

He went down on a knobbly knee,
And asked, "Pray, will you marry me?"
Fiona smiled and said, "No way!
But we can still be friends, okay?"

With bits of broken drumstick then
She made a brand new sword for Ben.
The ending? Well, for ever after,
They just got dafter and dafter and dafter!

The Battle of Brighton

Tell me, tell me, Grandad,
How off you went to war,
And fought the Battle of Brighton
In 1964!

Well, we rode down on our scooters
On that Bank Holiday,
We tooted on our hooters
And folk got out the way!

    Our headlamps were a-gleaming,
    Our mirrors, they were too.
    On each and every aerial
    A Union Jack we flew.

Now, when we got to Brighton,
And went along the prom,
There came a horde of Rockers,
Lord only knows where from!

I'll tell you of them Rockers,
They drove us up the pole,
'Cos we liked Motown music
While they dug rock 'n' roll.

And up against that rabble,
They weren't a pretty sight,
With slicked back hair and sideburns,
And ready for a fight.

It started just with jeering
And lots of huffs and puffs,
And then all of a sudden,
It came to fisticuffs!

We set about them Rockers,
(We didn't know no fear!),
We pelted them with pebbles
And chased them up the pier.

But as I grabbed one greaser,
His girlfriend took offence:
She hit me on my helmet
And left a lot of dents.

I fell, but that fair lady,
She held me in her arms,
She cradled me and told me
She hadn't meant no harm.

'Twas then I had a vision
And saw that it was wrong
To pick a fight with someone
When folk should rub along.

We slipped away together
(She gave her boy the boot),
With her dressed in her leathers
And me in my mod suit.

And being with that woman,
My new life soon began.
The next year we got married,
That girl is now your Nan.

Thank you, thank you, Grandad,
For telling me once more
Of how you met my granny
in 1964!

Ye Olde Ballade of Robin Hood

O, Robin Hood lived in a wood
Amongst the elms and oaks,
And every day he'd laugh and play
With lots of funny blokes …

… like Little John …

… and
Miller's
son,
(a tiny
lad
called
Much) …

… Alan-a-Dale …

… and Scarlet (Will) …

… and tubby
Friar Tuck.

One female fan,
Maid Marian,
Would join them
now and then,
And in a glade they
danced and swayed
Until one Wednesday
when …

… the Council came along and chopped down
all the trees and covered the place in concrete
and built a GINORMOUS multi-storey car park.

THE END